A Defense of the Nicene Definition

Also by BL. JOHN HENRY NEWMAN
Published by Assumption Press

NONFICTION

The Arians of the Fourth Century

An Essay in Aid of a Grammaar of Assent

An Essay on the Development of Christian Doctrine

The Idea of a Univeristy

Faith and Prejudice:
Catholic Sermons of Bl. John Henry Newman

FICTION

The Dream of Gerontius

Callista: A Tale of the Third Century

A DEFENSE OF THE NICENE DEFINITION

"DE DECRETIS"

BY
St. Athanasius

TRANSLATED BY
Bl. John Henry Newman

2014

Newman's translation of *A Defense of the Nicene Definition* was
originally published in *Select Treatises of St. Athanasius*, by James Parker
and Co. in1842. A revised edition was published Longmans, Green,
and Co. in 1881. This edition follows the 1881 edition with some
additional material from the 1842 version.

Cover image: *The Council of Nicaea*, Artist Unknown.

Contents

Epistle of Athanasius in Defense of the Nicene Definition of the Homoousion

(De Decretis)

Prefatory Notice

We have no means of determining the date of this Epistle, and critics do but offer conjectures at variance with each other. The Bollandists consider it to be earlier than A.D. 347, if not soon after the Nicene Council, e.g. 330 (Vit. Athan. c. 26). Montfaucon assigns some time between 350 and 354. Tillemont between 342 and 361.

Other aids towards determining it are such as these: it was written in a time of peace, after the experience and with the anticipation of persecution; but from 325 to 330 there was no such experience, from 330 to 347 no peace, and from 352 to 361 severe persecution; what interval is left for the date is from 348 to 352, which fulfils the requisite conditions, as being an interval of peace, with persecution before and after it.

It may be added that the rise of the Anomœans was about A.D. 350, and about the same time Acacius became the leader of the Eusebian or court party on the tactic in controversy of confining definitions of doctrine to Scripture language, and thereby virtually of annihilating dogmatic faith. Now the main topic and the occasion of this Epistle, as Athanasius shows again and again, is the revival of Arianism proper in its original outspoken vigour, the prominence of Acacius, and the appeal to Scripture against orthodoxy by him and other successors of Eusebius.

J.H.N.

Chapter One

INTRODUCTION

The complaint of the Arians against the Nicene Council; their fickleness; they are like Jews; their employment of force instead of reason.

1. THOU HAST DONE WELL, in signifying to me the discussion thou hast had with the advocates of Arianism, among whom were certain of the party of Eusebius, as well as very many of the brethren who hold the doctrine of the Church. Very welcome to me was thy Christian vigilance, which excellently confuted the impiety of their heresy; while I marvelled at the effrontery which led them, after the exposures already made of their bad reasonings in the past, and of that perverse temper to which all men bore witness, still to be complaining like the Jews, "Why did the bishops at Nicæa use terms not in Scripture, 'Of the substance' and 'Consubstantial'?" Thou then, as a man of learning, in spite of their pretences, didst convict them of talking idly; and they

3

in those pretences were but acting in accordance with their own evil disposition. For they are as variable and fickle in their sentiments, as chameleons in their colours; and when confuted they are confused; and when questioned they hesitate; and then they lose shame, and betake themselves to evasions. Lastly, when detected in these, they do not rest till they have invented fresh pleas which have no substance, and all this that they may persist in being loyal to an impiety.

2. Now such tactics are nothing else than an obvious token of their want of Divine Reason, and a copying, as I have said, of Jewish malignity. For the Jews too, when convicted by the Truth, and unable to confront it, made excuses, such as *What miracles doest Thou, that we may see and believe Thee? What dost Thou work?*[1] though so many miracles were given, that they themselves said, *What do we? for this man doeth many miracles?*[2] In truth, dead men were raised, lame walked, blind saw afresh, lepers were cleansed, and the water became wine, and five loaves satisfied five thousand, and all of them wondered and worshipped the Lord, confessing that in Him were fulfilled the prophecies, and that He was God, the Son of God; all but the Pharisees, who, though the miracles shone brighter than the sun, yet complained still, as ignorant men, *Why dost Thou, being*

---

[1] John 6:30
[2] John 11:47

4

a man, make Thyself God?[3] Insensate, and verily blind in understanding! they ought contrariwise to have said, "Why hast Thou, being God, become man?" for His works did prove Him God, that thereupon they might both worship the Father's goodness, and admire the Son's descent from on high for our sakes. However, this they did not say; no, nor would they witness what He was doing; or they witnessed indeed, for this they could not avoid, but they changed their ground of complaint and said again, "Why healest Thou the paralytic, why makest Thou the born-blind to see, on the sabbath day?" But this too was a mere excuse and a finding fault; for on other days as well as the sabbath did the Lord heal *all manner of sickness, and all manner of disease,*[4] but they complained still according to their wont, and in calling Him Beelzebub, preferred the imputation of Atheism, to a recantation of their wickedness. And though *in sundry times and diverse manners*[5] the Saviour thus showed His own Godhead and preached the Father to all men, nevertheless, as kicking against the goad, they rashly spoke against Him, as if in order that, according to the divine proverb, they might find *occasions for separating themselves*[6] from the truth.

---

[3] John 10:33

[4] Matt 4:23

[5] Heb 1:1

[6] Prov 18:1

3. As then the Jews of that day, for acting thus wickedly and denying the Lord, were with justice deprived of their laws and of the promise made to their fathers, so the Arians, judaizing now, are in my judgment in circumstances like those of Caiaphas and the contemporary Pharisees. For, perceiving that their heresy is utterly unreasonable, they start difficulties, saying, "Why was this defined and not that?" Yet wonder not though in the event they do not persevere in that sort of warfare; for in no long time they will have recourse to outrage, and will be throwing out threats of *the band and the captain.*[7] Such is their inconsistency; yet how can it be otherwise with them? for, denying the Word of God, Divine Reason they have utterly forfeited. Aware then of this, I would of myself have made no reply to their attacks; but, since thy friendliness has asked to know what was done in the Council, I have not delayed to inform you, in order to show in few words how destitute Arianism is of a religious temper, and how its very business is to frame evasions.

---

[7] John 18:12

Chapter Two

Conduct of the Arians toward the Nicene Council

Ignorant as well as irreligious to attempt to reverse an Ecumenical Council; proceedings at Nicæa; Eusebians then signed what they now complain of; on the unanimity of true teachers and the process of tradition; changes of the Arians.

4. AND DO THOU, beloved, consider whether it be not so. If, the devil having sown their hearts with this perverseness, they are so confident in the truth of their reasonings, why do they not first clear themselves of the charge of heresy which lies against them? and then will come the time for them to criticise the definition of the Council. For no one, on being convicted of murder or adultery, is at liberty after the trial to arraign the sentence of the judge, why he spoke in this way and not in that. For this, instead of exculpating the convict, rather increases his crime on the score of petulance and audacity. Why did not they find fault with the wording of the definition at the time when it was framed? but now when their first duty is to repeat after the Council

those anathemas in which its creed ends, instead of this, they profess to have scruples as to the creed itself, and they find matter for a subterfuge in the fact, which no one denies, that the word "substance" is not in Scripture. Surely it is just that those who are under a charge should confine themselves to their own defence. While their own conscience is so unclean, they are not quite the men to quarrel with an act which in truth they do not understand. Rather, let them investigate the matter in a docile spirit, and, in order to learn what hitherto they had not known, let them cleanse their ears in the stream of truth and the doctrine of piety.

5. Now it happened to the Eusebians in the Nicene Council in this wise:—On their making a stand in behalf of their impiety, the assembled bishops, who were more or less three hundred in number, mildly and courteously called upon them to explain and defend themselves. Scarcely, however, did they begin to speak, when they pronounced their own condemnation, for one differed from another; then, perceiving the serious straits in which their heresy lay, they remained dumb, and by their silence confessed the disgrace which came upon them. On this the Bishops, after condemning the formulæ which they had devised, published against them the sound and ecclesiastical faith; and, whereas all subscribed it, the Eusebians subscribed it too in those very phrases, of which they are now complaining, (I mean, "Of the substance," and "Consubstantial,") professing that

"the Son of God is neither creature nor work, nor in the number of things made from nothing, but that the Word is an Offspring from the substance of the Father." And, what is strange indeed, Eusebius of Cæsarea in Palestine, who had refused the day before, yet afterwards subscribed, and sent to his church a letter, saying that this was the Church's faith and the tradition of the Fathers; and thereby made it clear to all that his party were in error before, and were rashly contending against the truth. For, though he was ashamed at the moment to adopt these phrases, and excused himself to his Church in his own way, yet he certainly means to signify his acceptance of them, in that he does not in his Epistle deny the "One in substance," and "Consubstantial." And in this way he got into a difficulty; for, in excusing himself, he thereby was attacking the Arians, as if their stating that "the Son was not before His generation," was their denial of His existence even before His birth in the flesh. And Acacius too knows this well, though he also through fear may pretend otherwise because of the times, and may deny the fact. Accordingly I have subjoined at the end of these remarks the letter of Eusebius, that thou mayst know from it the scanty regard shown by Christ's enemies towards their own masters, and singularly by Acacius himself.

6. Are they not then committing a crime, in their very thought to gainsay the decree of so great and ecumenical a Council? are they not in transgression, when they dare to

confront that good definition against Arianism, acknowledged, as it was, by those who had in the first instance taught them their impiety? And supposing, even after subscription, Eusebius and his did change again, and return like *dogs to their own vomit*[8] of impiety, then surely the present gainsayers do but deserve still greater detestation, for they are sacrificing their souls' liberty to those, as the masters of their heresy, who are, as James has said, *double-minded men, and unstable in all their ways,*[9] not having one opinion, but changing to and fro, and now recommending certain statements, but soon dishonouring them, and in turn recommending what just now they were blaming. But this, as the Shepherd has said, is to be "the child of the devil," and is the note of hucksters rather than of doctors. For, what our Fathers have of old delivered, this is really doctrine; and this truly the token of doctors, to confess the same thing with each other, and to vary neither from themselves nor from their fathers; whereas they who have not this character are not to be called true doctors but charlatans. Thus the Greeks, as not witnessing to the same doctrines, but quarrelling one with another, have no truth of teaching; but the holy and veritable heralds of the truth agree together, not differ. For though they lived in different times, yet they one

---

[8] Prov 26:11
[9] Jas 1:18

and all tend the same way, being prophets of the one God, and preaching the same Word harmoniously.

7. And thus what Moses taught, that Abraham kept; and what Abraham kept, that Noe and Enoch acknowledged, discriminating pure from impure, and becoming acceptable to God. For Abel too in this way witnessed unto death, taught in the truths which he had learned from Adam, who himself had learned from the Lord, and He again, when He came in the last age for the abolishment of sin, said, *I give no new commandment unto you.*[10] Wherefore also the blessed Apostle Paul, who had learnt it from Him, when he is determining ecclesiastical duties, forbade that even deacons, not to say bishops, should be *double-tongued*;[11] and in his rebuke of the Galatians, he made a broad declaration, *If any one preach any other Gospel unto you than that ye have received, let him be anathema. As I have said, so say I again; if even an Angel from Heaven should preach unto you any other gospel than that ye have received, let him be anathema.*[12]

8. Thus the Apostle. If then truth lay, as the Eusebians afterwards said, otherwise than their subscription implied, the present men ought to anathematise them for subscribing; if on the other hand they subscribed to a truth, what ground have they of complaint against the great Council which imposed

---

[10]   1 John 2:7
[11]   1 Tim 3:8
[12]   Gal 1:9-8

on them the subscription? But if they blame the Council's act, yet let off those who took part in it, they are themselves too plainly the sport of every wind and wave, and are influenced by opinions, not their own, but of others, and being such, are as little trustworthy now as before, in what they allege. Rather let them cease to carp at what they understand not; lest so it be that, not knowing to discriminate, they at hazard call evil good and good evil, and think that bitter is sweet and sweet bitter. Doubtless their real desire is that doctrines which have already been judged wrong and have been reprobated should gain the ascendancy, and they make violent efforts to prejudice what was rightly defined. Nor is there reason for further explanation on our part or answer to their excuses, nor for further resistance on theirs, instead of acquiescence in what the leaders of their heresy subscribed; but since, from an extraordinary want of modesty, the present men perhaps hope to be able to advocate an impiety, which really is from the Evil One, with better success than those who went before them, therefore, though in my former letter written to thee, I have already argued at length against them, notwithstanding, I am ready now also to examine each of their separate statements, as I did those of their predecessors; for now not less than then their heresy shall be shown to have no soundness in it, but to be a *doctrine of demons.*[13]

---

[13] 1 Tim 4:1

Chapter Three

THE MEANING OF THE WORD "SON" AS APPLIED TO OUR LORD

Two senses of the word, 1. adoptive; 2. substantial; attempts of Arians to find a third meaning between these; e.g. that our Lord only was created immediately by God; Asterius's view; or that our Lord alone partakes the Father. The second and true sense; God begets as He makes, really; though His creation and generation not like man's; His generation independent of time; generation implies an internal, and therefore an eternal, act in God; explanation of Prov. viii. 22.

9. THEY SAY then what the others held and dared to maintain before them: "Not always Father, always Son; for the Son was not before His generation, but, as others, came out of nothing; and in consequence God was not always Father of the Son; but when the Son came into being and was created, then was God called His Father. For the Word is a creature and work, and foreign and unlike to the Father in substance; and the Son is neither by nature the Father's true Word, nor His only and true Wisdom; but being a creature and one of the works, He is by an abuse of words called Word and Wisdom; for by the Word which is in God was

He made, as were all things. Wherefore the Son is not true God."

10. Now it may serve to bring home to them what they are saying, to ask them first this, what a son simply is, and of what is that name significant. In truth, Divine Scripture acquaints us with a double sense of this word:—one which Moses sets before us in the Law, *When thou shalt hearken to the voice of the Lord thy God, to keep all His commandments which I command thee this day, to do that which is right in the eyes of the Lord thy God, ye shall be children of the Lord your God;*[14] as also in the Gospel, John says, *But as many as received Him, to them gave He power to become the sons of God*[15]:—and the other sense is that in which Isaac is son of Abraham, and Jacob of Isaac, and the Patriarchs of Jacob. Now in which of these two senses, literal or figurative, do they understand the Son of God in such figments as the foregoing? for I feel sure they will issue in the same impiety as the Eusebians.

11. First, let us suppose the word Son to be taken in the figurative, not the literal sense; and this is how they really understand it (as their predecessors did), only many of them shrink from saying so. If this is the sense in which the title "Son of God" is to be taken, then I observe, first of

---

[14] Deut 13:18; 14:1

[15] John 1:12

all, that sonship in this sense is a grace gained from above by those who have made progress in goodness, and who receive *power to become sons of God*; and then, if so, He would surely in nothing differ from us, who are also born of God; no, nor would He be Only-begotten, as having obtained the title of Son, as others have, from His virtue. For granting what they say, that, whereas His qualifications were foreknown, He, on that account, from His very first beginning, by anticipation, received the name, and the glory of the name, still there will be no difference between Him and those who receive the name for their actions, so long as this is the ground on which He as others is recognised as Son. For Adam too, though he received grace from the first, and upon his creation was at once placed in paradise, differed in no respect either from Enoch, who was translated thither after his birth on his pleasing God, or from the Apostle, who also was caught up to paradise after his good actions; nay, nor from the thief, who, by virtue of his confession, received a promise that he should be forthwith in paradise.

12. Next when thus pressed, they will perhaps make an answer which has brought them into difficulty many times already: "We consider that the Son has this prerogative over other beings, and therefore is called Only-begotten, because He alone was brought into being by God alone, and all other things were created by God through the Son." Now I wonder who it was that suggested to you so futile and novel

an idea as that the Father alone wrought with His own hand the Son alone, and that all other things were brought into being by the Son as by an under-worker. If for the toil-sake God was content with making the Son only, instead of making all things at once, this is an impious thought, especially in the case of those who know the words of Esaias, *The everlasting God, the Lord, the Creator of the ends of the earth, hungereth not, neither is weary; there is no searching of His understanding.*[16] Rather it is He who to the hungry gives strength, and through His word refreshes the labouring. On the other hand it is impious to suppose that He disdained, as if a humble task, Himself to form the creatures which came into being after the Son; for there is no pride in that God, who goes down with Jacob into Egypt, and for Abraham's sake corrects Abimelec in behalf of Sara, and speaks face to face with Moses, who was but a man, and descends upon Mount Sinai, and by His secret grace fights for the people against Amalec. However, you are false in your fact, for we are told, *He made us, and not we ourselves.*[17] He it is that, through His Word, made all things small and great, and we may not divide the creation, and say this is the Father's, and this is the Son's, but all things are of one God, who uses His proper Word as a Hand, and in Him does all things. As God

---

[16]   Isa 40:28
[17]   Ps 100:3

Himself shows us, when He says, *All these things hath My Hand made*;[18] and Paul taught us as he had been taught, that *There is One God, from whom are all things; and One Lord Jesus Christ, through whom are all things.*[19] Thus He, always as now, speaks to the sun and it rises, and commands the clouds and it rains upon one place, and another, where it does not rain, is dried up. And He bids the earth to give its fruit, and fashions Jeremias in the womb. But if He now does all this, assuredly at the beginning also He did not disdain through the Word to make all things Himself; for these are but parts of the whole.

18. But now, thirdly, let us suppose, as sometimes has been said, that the other creatures could not endure to be wrought by the direct Hand of the Ingenerate, and therefore the Son alone was brought into being by the Father alone, and other things by the Son as an under-worker and assistant, for this is what Asterius the sacrificer has written, and what Arius has transcribed and bequeathed to his own friends; and from that time they used this formula, broken reed as it is, being ignorant, the bewildered men, of its rottenness. For if it was impossible for things created to bear the hand of God, and you hold the Son to be one of their number, how was even He equal to this formation by God alone?

---

18   Isa 66:2
19   1 Cor 8:6

and if an intermediate was necessary that things that came into being might come, and you hold the Son to be one of such, then must there have been some medium before Him, for His own creation; and, that intermediate himself again being a creature, it follows that he too needed another Mediator for his own framing. And though we were to devise another, we must still first devise his Mediator, so that we shall never come to an end. And thus a Mediator being ever in request, never would the creation be constituted, because nothing that has come into being can, as you say, bear the direct hand of the Ingenerate. And if, on your perceiving the extravagance of this, you begin to say that the Son, though a creature, was made capable of being made immediately by the Ingenerate, then all the other things also, though they are mere creatures, are capable of being framed immediately by the Ingenerate; for the Son too is but a creature in your judgment, as everything else. And consequently the generation of the Word is superfluous, according to your impious and futile imagination, God being sufficient for the immediate formation of all things, and all things that have been brought out of nothing being capable of sustaining His direct hand.

14. These impious men then having so little mind amid their madness, let us see, fourthly, whether this particular sophism will not prove even more irrational than the others. Adam was created alone by God alone (through the Word);

yet no one would say that Adam differed from those who came after him in having thereby something in his nature more than all other men (granting that he alone was made by God alone, and that we all spring from Adam and consist by succession of our race) so long as we consider him fashioned from the earth as others, and that, at first not existing, he afterwards came to be. But though we were to allow some prerogative to the Protoplast as having been formed by the very Hand of God, still it must be accounted to him as one of honour, not of nature. For he came of the earth, as all other men; and the Hand which then fashioned Adam, now also and ever is fashioning and giving entire consistence to those who come after him. And God Himself declares this to Jeremias, as I said before: *Before I formed thee in the womb, I knew thee;*[20] and so He says of all, *All those things hath My hand made;*[21] and again by Esaias, *Thus saith the Lord, thy Redeemer, and He that formed thee from the womb; I am the Lord that maketh all things, that stretcheth forth the heavens alone, that spreadeth abroad the earth by Myself.*[22] And David, knowing this, says in the Psalm, *Thy Hands have made me and fashioned me;*[23] and he who says in Esaias, *Thus saith the Lord who formed me from the womb to*

---

[20] Jer 1:5

[21] Isa 66:2

[22] Isa 44:24

[23] Job 10:8; Ps 119:73

be His servant,[24] signifies the same. Therefore, in respect of nature, he differs nothing from us though he precedes us in time, so long as we all consist and are created by the same Hand. If then these be your thoughts, O Arians, about the Son of God also, that thus He subsists and came to be, then in your judgment He will differ nothing on the score of nature from others, supposing He too once was not, and then was brought into being, and the name of Son was, on His creation, for His virtue's sake, by grace united to Him. For, from what you say, He Himself is one of those of whom the Spirit says in the Psalms, *He spake the word and they were made; He commanded and they were created.*[25] If so, who was it to whom God gave command for the Son's creation? for a Word there must be to whom God *gave command*, and in whom the works are *created*; but ye have no other to show than the Word whom ye deny, unless indeed you should again devise some new notion.

15. "Yes," they will say, "we have found another;" (which indeed I have formerly heard from the Eusebians,) "on this score do we consider that the Son of God has a prerogative over others, and is called Only-begotten, because He alone partakes the Father, and all other things partake the Son." Thus they weary themselves in changing and varying their

---

[24] Isa 49:5

[25] Ps 33:9

statements, like so many pigments; however, this shall not save them from an exposure, as men who speak empty words out of the earth, and wallow as if in the mire of their own devices. For if indeed He were called God's Son, and we the Son's sons, their fiction were plausible; but if we too are said to be sons of that God, of whom He is Son, then we too partake the Father, who says, *I have begotten and exalted children.*[26] For, if we did not partake Him, He had not said, *I have begotten*; but, if He Himself begat us, no other than He is our Father. And, as before, it avails not, whether the Son has something more and was made first, whereas we have something less and were made afterwards, as long as we all partake, and are called sons, of the same Father. For the more or less does not indicate a different nature; but attaches to each according to the practice of virtue; and one is placed over ten cities, another over five; and some sit on twelve thrones judging the twelve tribes of Israel; and others hear the words, *Come, ye blessed of My Father,*[27] and, *Well done, good and faithful servant.*[28] With these ideas, however, no wonder they imagine that of such a Son God was not always Father, and that such a Son was not always in existence, but was brought into being from nothing, as a creature, and was not before His generation; for such a one is other than the True Son of God.

---

[26] Isa 1:2

[27] Matt 25:34

[28] Matt 21:23

16. But to persist in thus speaking involves guilt; for it is the tone of thought of Sadducees, and of Samosatene to consider that the Word and Wisdom of the Father is but His Son by grace and adoption: it remains then to say that He is Son in the second of the senses above specified, viz., not by an extreme figure, but in a literal sense, as Isaac was son of Abraham as being begotten of him. In other words, the Son is of the nature of the Father, for nature and nothing short of nature is implied in the idea of sonship, generation, or derivation. A son is a father's increase, not acquisition; from within not from without. I know the objection which will be made to this doctrine; it will be said that I have proposed a mere human conception of a sacred truth, altogether earthly and utterly unworthy of God, but I cannot accept such an account of it. Such an objection only argues ignorance in those who make it; for analogy does not involve likeness. Spirit is not as body, God is not as man, nor man as God. Men are created of matter, and their substance is liable to increase and loss; but God is immortal and incorporeal. And if so be the same terms are used of God and of man in divine Scripture, yet the clear-sighted, as Paul injoins, will study its text and thereby discriminate, and dispose of what is written there according to the nature of each subject, and will avoid any confusion of sense, so as not to conceive of the attributes of God in a human way, nor again to ascribe the properties of man to God. For this were to mix wine with

water, and to place upon the altar strange fire together with that which is divine.

17. For instance, God creates, and man too is said to create, and God has being, and men too are said to be. Yet does God create as man does? or has He being as man has being? Perish the thought; we understand the terms in one sense of God, and in another of men. For God creates in that He calls into being that which is not, needing nothing thereunto: but men create by working some existing material, first praying, and thereby gaining the science to execute from that God who has framed all things by His proper Word. And again, men, being incapable of self-existence, are inclosed in place, and have their consistence in the Word of God; but God is self-existent, inclosing all things, and inclosed by none; within all according to His own goodness and power, yet without all in His proper nature. As then men create not as God creates, as their being is not such as God's being, so men's generation is in one way, and the Son is from the Father in another. For the offsprings of men are in some sort portions of their fathers, since the very nature of bodies is to be compounded and dissoluble, and to act by piecemeal; and men lose their substance in begetting, and again they gain substance from the accession of food. And on this account men in their time become fathers of many children; but God, who is individual, is Father of the Son without being parted or affected, for there is neither loss nor

gain to the Immaterial, as there is in the case of men, and, being simple in His nature, He gives absolutely and utterly all that He is, and thereby is Father of One Only Son. This is why the Son is Only-begotten, and alone in the Father's bosom, and alone is acknowledged by the Father to be from Him, as in the words, *This is My beloved Son, in whom I am well pleased*.[29] And therefore also, He is the Father's Word, a title which suggests that the Divine Nature is beyond liability to affection and division, in that not even a human word is begotten with any such accidents, much less the Word of God. Wherefore, also, He sits, as Word, at the Father's right hand; for where the Father is, there also is His Word; but we, as being His works, stand in judgment before Him; and He is adored, because He is Son of the adorable Father, but we adore, confessing Him Lord and God, because we are creatures and other than He.

18. If this be so, we come to this question:—supposing by the appellation of Son of God must be meant God's offspring, the fulness of His very Self, can it be a light sin, to maintain that He was made out of nothing, and was not before His generation? It is of course a subject which transcends the thoughts of men, but, I repeat, God's nature is not bound by the conditions of ours. We become fathers of our children in time, but God, in that He ever is, is ever Fa-

---

[29] Matt 3:17

ther of His Son. And the generation of mankind is familiarised to us from earthly instances that are parallel; but since *no one knoweth the Son but the Father, and no one knoweth the Father but the Son, and he to whomsoever the Son will reveal Him,*[30] therefore the sacred writers, to whom the Son has revealed Him, have given us a sort of image, but nothing more, from things visible, saying, *Who is the brightness of His glory and the impress of His Person;*[31] and again, *For with Thee is the well of life, and in Thy light shall we see light;*[32] and when the Word chides Israel, He says, *Thou hast forsaken the Fountain of wisdom;*[33] and this Fountain it is which says, *They have forsaken Me, the Fountain of living waters.*[34] And mean indeed and very dim is the illustration compared with what we desiderate; but yet it is possible from it to understand something above man's nature, instead of thinking the Son's generation to be on a level with ours. For instance, who can even imagine that the radiance of light "once was not," so that he should dare to say that "the Son was not always," or that "the Son was not before His generation"? or who is capable of separating the radiance from the sun, or of conceiving of the Fountain

---

[30] Matt 11:27

[31] Heb 1:3

[32] Ps 36:9

[33] Bar 3:12

[34] Jer 2:13

as ever void of life, that he should say, even if mad, "The Son is from nothing," (who says Himself, *I am the life*[35]), or "alien to the Father's substance," (who says, *He that hath seen Me hath seen the Father?*[36]) for the sacred writers wishing us thus to understand, have given these illustrations; and it is irrelevant and most impious, when Scripture contains such images, to form ideas concerning our Lord from others which are neither in Scripture, nor have any pious bearing.

19. Let us go by Scripture; then from what teacher or by what tradition have you derived these notions about the Saviour? From what passages of Scripture? "Yes," they will say, "in the Proverbs we read, *The Lord hath created Me a beginning of His ways unto His works.*[37] This the Eusebians used to insist upon in former years, and you write me word that the present men also, though overthrown and confuted by an abundance of proof, still are putting about in every quarter this passage, and saying that the Son is one of the creatures, and reckoning Him with things which came into being out of nothing. But I answer first, it cannot mean this, supposing we have already proved Him to be a Son. Son and creature are ideas incompatible with each other. If then Son, therefore not creature: if creature, not Son: for vast is the difference between them, and Son and creature

---

[35] John 11:25; 14:6
[36] John 14:9
[37] Prov 8:22

cannot be the same, unless His substance be considered to be at once from God and yet external to God. This at first sight; but, secondly, these men seem to me to have a wrong understanding of this passage. They ask us again and again, like so many noisy gnats, "Has the passage no meaning?" Yes, it has a meaning, a pious and very orthodox meaning, but not theirs, and had they understood it, they would not have blasphemed the *Lord of glory*.[38] It is true to say that the Son was created, but this took place when He became man; for creation belongs to man. And any one may find this sense duly conveyed in the divine oracles, who, instead of accounting their perusal a secondary matter, investigates the time and persons, and the purpose, and thus studies and ponders what he reads. Now as to the season spoken of, he will find for certain that, whereas the Lord always exists, at length in fulness of the ages He became man; and whereas He is Son of God, He became Son of man also. And as to the need he will understand that, wishing to annul our death, He took on Himself a body from the Virgin Mary; in order that, by offering this unto the Father a sacrifice for all, He might deliver us all, who by fear of death were *all our life through subject to bondage*.[39] And as to the person, this is indeed the Saviour's, but it is then said of Him when He

---

[38] 1 Cor 2:8
[39] Heb 2:15

took a body and said, *The Lord has created Me a beginning of His ways unto His works*. For as it properly belongs to Him, as God's Son, to be everlasting, and to be in the Father's bosom, so, on His becoming man, the words befitted Him, *The Lord created Me*. For then they are said of Him, and then He hungered, and thirsted, and asked where Lazarus lay, and suffered, and rose again. And as, when we hear of Him as Lord and God and true Light, we understand Him as being from the Father, so on hearing *The Lord created*, and *Servant*, and *He suffered*, we shall justly ascribe this, not to His Godhead, for it does not belong to It, but we must interpret it of that flesh which He bore for our sakes; for to it these things are proper, and this flesh itself was none other's than the Word's. And if we wish to know the advantages we attain by this, we shall find them to be as follows: that the Word was made flesh, not only to offer up this body for all, but that we, partaking of His Spirit, might be made gods, a gift which we could not otherwise have gained than by His clothing Himself in our created body; for hence we derive our name of "men of God" and "men in Christ." And as we, by receiving the Spirit, do not lose our own proper substance, so the Lord, when made man for us, and bearing a body, was no less God; for He was not lessened by the envelopment of the body, but rather deified it and rendered it immortal.

Chapter Four

THE OMNIPOTENCE OF GOD THE REASON FOR FAITH AND HOPE

Power, Word or Reason, and Wisdom, the names of the Son,
imply eternity; as well as the Father's title of Fountain. The
Arians reply that these do not formally belong to the essence of
the Son, but are names given Him; that God has many words,
powers, &c. Why there is but one Son and Word, &c. All the
titles of the Son coincide in Him.

20. THIS THEN is quite enough in order to denounce as infamous this Arian heresy; for, as the Lord has granted, out of their own words is impiety brought home to them. But now let us on our part act on the offensive, and call on them for an answer; for it is fair time, when their own ground has failed them, to question them on ours; perhaps it may abash the perverse, and make them see whence they have fallen. It has been shown above that the appellation "Son" is so far from implying beginning of existence as actually to suggest co-existence and co-eternity and co-divinity with God the Father. But, besides this, I have incidentally referred to the passages in Holy Scripture which speak of our Lord as the Divine Word and Wisdom, and

the meaning of these titles, when carefully considered, is a confirmation that He is truly and literally the Son. The Apostle, for instance, says, *Christ the Power of God and the Wisdom of God*;[40] and John after saying, *and the Word was made flesh*, at once adds, *And we have seen His glory the glory as of the Only-begotten of the Father full of grace and truth*;[41] so that, the Word being the Only-begotten Son, is also that Power and that Wisdom by which heaven and earth and all that is therein were made. In like manner we have learnt from Baruch that Wisdom comes from a Fountain, and that that Fountain is God; what then is Wisdom but His Son? Now, if they deny Scripture, they are at once aliens from the Christian name, and may fitly be called of all men atheists, and Christ's enemies, for they have brought upon themselves these titles. But if they agree with us that the sayings of Scripture are divinely inspired, let them dare to say openly what they think in secret, that the Word and Wisdom being the Son, the Word and Wisdom of the Father had a beginning, that is, that God was once wordless and wisdomless; and let them in their madness say, "There was once when He was not," and "before His generation, Christ was not;" and again let them declare that the Fountain begat not Wisdom from Itself, but

---

[40] 1 Cor 1:24
[41] John 1:14

acquired It from without, till they have the daring to say, "The Son came of nothing;" whence it will follow that His origin is no longer a Fountain, but a sort of pool, as if merely receiving water from without, and usurping the name of Fountain.

21. How full of impiety this is, I consider none can doubt who has ever so little understanding; however, they shall be answered as Arius was, and as I noticed when I began. They whisper something about titles, Word and Wisdom are titles of the Son, only titles; titles! then what is His real name? What is He really? is He more than those titles, or less than them? If He is greater than the titles, it is not lawful from the lesser to designate the higher, but, if He be in His own nature less than the titles, then it follows that He has earned what is higher than His original self, and this implies in Him a moral advance, which is an impiety equal to anything that has gone before. For that He who is in the Father, and in whom also the Father is, who says, *I and the Father are one,*[42] whom *he that hath seen, hath seen the Father,*[43] to imply, I say, by the titles you give Him that He has been improved by anything external, is the extreme of madness.

22. However, when they are beaten hence, and like the

---

[42] John 10:30
[43] John 14:9

old Eusebians are in these great straits, then they have this remaining plea, which Arius too in ballads, and in his own Thalia, fabled, starting it as a new difficulty: "Many words speaketh God; which then of these are we to call Son and Word, Only-begotten of the Father?" Insensate, and anything but Christians! for first, in using such language about God, they are not far from conceiving of Him as a man, who speaks and then modifies His first words by His second, just as if one Word from God were not sufficient for the framing of all things at the Father's will, and for His providential care of all. For His speaking many words would argue a feebleness in them all, each needing the service of the other. But that God should act through One Word, which is the true doctrine, both shows the power of God, and the perfection of the Word that is from Him, and the pious understanding of them who thus believe.

23. O that they would be led to confess the truth from these their own admissions now! how near they come to it, in order to start off again in hopeless divergence! They grant that "many words speaketh God," and what is such utterance but in some sort a bringing forth? He is a Father of words; then why not in that way which is most perfect? why not rather the Father of One Word than of many?—of a Word substantive and from His own fulness rather than of mere utterances which come and go and have no stay? These men are loth to say that there is no substantial Word

of God, why then do they not go on to confess that that Word is a Son also? Is Son a mere title without substance? and must not also that Word be a reflection or image? and, as God is One, is not His Image substantive and one? and who is that but the One Son? All these appellations look to one Object, and each of them subserves the rest. For the Son of God, as may be learnt from the divine oracles themselves, is Himself the Word of God, and the Wisdom, and the Image, and the Hand, and the Power; for God's Offspring is One, and of the generation from the Father these titles are tokens. If you say the Son, you have declared what is from the Father by nature; and if you imagine the Word, you are thinking again of what is from Him, and what is inseparable; and speaking of Wisdom, again you mean in like manner, what is not from without, but from Him and in Him; and if you name the Power and the Hand, again you speak of what is proper to the substance; and, speaking of the Image, you signify the Son; for what else is like God but the Offspring from Him? Doubtless the things which came into being through *the Word*, these are *founded in Wisdom*;[44] and what are *founded in Wisdom*, these are all made by the *Hand*, and came to be through the Son.

24. And we have proof of this, not from adventitious authorities, but from the Scriptures; for God Himself says

---

[44] Prov 3:19

by Esaias the Prophet, *My Hand also hath laid the foundation of the earth, and My right Hand hath spanned the heavens.* And again, *And I have covered them in the shadow of My Hand, that I may plant the heavens and lay the foundations of the earth.*[45] And David being taught this, and knowing that the Lord's Hand was nothing else than Wisdom, says in the Psalm, *In Wisdom hast Thou made them all; the earth is full of Thy riches.*[46] Solomon also received the same from God, and said, *The Lord by Wisdom hath founded the earth;*[47] and John knowing that the Word was the Hand and the Wisdom, thus preaches the gospel, *In the beginning was the Word and the Word was with God and the Word was God; the same was in the beginning with God: all things were made by Him, and without Him was not anything made.*[48] And the Apostle, understanding that the Hand and the Wisdom and the Word was nothing else than the Son, says *God who at sundry times and in divers manners spake in time past unto the Fathers by the Prophets, hath in these last days spoken unto us by His Son, whom He hath appointed Heir of all things, by whom also He made the ages.*[49] And

---

[45] Isa 48:13
[46] Ps 104:24
[47] Prov 3:19
[48] John 1:1-3
[49] Heb 1:1-2

again, *There is One Lord Jesus Christ, through whom are all things, and we through Him.*[50] And knowing also that the Word, the Wisdom, the Son was the Image Himself of the Father, he says in the Epistle to the Colossians, *Giving thanks to God and the Father which hath made us meet to be partakers of the inheritance of the saints in light, who hath delivered us from the power of darkness, and hath translated us into the kingdom of His dear Son; in whom we have redemption, even the remission of sins; who is the Image of the Invisible God the First-born of every creature; for by Him were all things created, that are in heaven and that are in earth, visible and invisible, whether they be thrones, or dominions, or principalities, or powers; all things were created by Him and for Him: and He is before all things, and in Him all things consist.*[51]

25. For as all things are created by the Word, so, because He is the Image, are they also created in Him. And thus a man who directs his thoughts to the Lord will be saved from stumbling upon the stone of offence, and will go forward to that illumination which streams from the light of truth; for this is really the sentiment of piety, though these contentious men burst with spite, neither devout towards God, nor abashed by the arguments which confute them.

---

[50]   1 Cor 8:6
[51]   Col 1:12-16

A Defense of the Nicene Definition

DEFENCE OF THE COUNCIL'S PHRASES, "ONE IN SUBSTANCE" AND "OF THE SUBSTANCE

Objection that the phrases are not scriptural; we ought to look at the sense more than the wording; evasion of the Eusebians as to the phrase "of God" which is in Scripture; their evasion of all explanations but those which the Council selected; which were intended to negative the Arian formulæ; protest against their conveying any material sense.

26. Now THE EUSEBIANS were at that former time examined at great length, and passed sentence on themselves, as I said before; on this they subscribed; and after this change of mind they kept in quiet and retirement; but since the present party, in the wantonness of impiety, and in their wild vagaries about the truth, are full set upon accusing the Council, let them tell us, I repeat, what is the sort of Scriptures from which they have learned, or who is the Saint by whom they have been taught, to heap together their phrases, "Out of nothing," and "He was not before His generation," and "Once He was not," and "Alterable," and the "Pre-existence," and "At God's will;" which are their fables in mockery of the Lord. Considering then that they on their part

37

have made use of phrases not in Scripture, and that with a view thereby of expressing impious notions, it does not become them to find fault with those who for a pious purpose go beyond Scripture. Disguise it as you will by artful terms and plausible sophisms, impiety is a sin; but represent the truth under ever so strange a formula, while it is truth, it at least is piety. That what these Christ-opposers advanced was impious falsehood, I have proved both now and formerly; that what the Council defined was pious truth is equally clear, as will be granted by any careful inquirer into the occasion of the definition. It was as follows:—

27. The Council wishing to condemn the impious phrases of the Arians, and to use instead the received terms of Scripture, namely, that the Son is not from nothing, but *from God*, and is the *Word* and *Wisdom* and not a creature or work, but the proper Offspring from the Father, the party of Eusebius, out of their inveterate heterodoxy, understood the phrase *from God* as common to Him and to us, as if in respect to it the Word of God differed nothing from us, and this, because it is written, *There is One God from whom all things*;[52] and again, *Old things are passed away, behold all things are new, and all things are from God*.[53] But the Fathers, perceiving their craft and the cunning of their im-

---

[52] 1 Cor 8:6
[53] 2 Cor 5:17-18

piety, were forced thereupon to express more distinctly the sense of the words *from God*. Accordingly, they wrote "from the substance of God," in order that *from God* might not be considered common and equal in the Son and in things which are made, but that all others might be acknowledged as creatures, and the Word alone as from the Father. For though all things be said to be from God, yet this is not in the sense in which the Son is from Him; for as to the creatures, "*from God*" is said of them, in that they exist not at random or spontaneously, nor come into being by chance, according to those philosophers who refer them to the combination of atoms, and to elements which are homogeneous, nor as certain heretics imagine some other Framer, nor as others again say that the constitution of all things is from certain Angels; not for these reasons, but because, whereas there is a God, it was by Him that all things were brought into being, when as yet they were not, through His Word; and as to the Word, since He is not a creature, He alone is really, as well as is called, *from the Father*; and this is signified, when it is said that the Son is "from the substance of the Father," for to no creature does this attach. In truth, when Paul says that *all things are from God*, he immediately adds, *and one Lord, Jesus Christ, through whom all things*,[54] by way of showing all men that the Son is other than all these things which

---

[54] 1 Cor 8:6

came into being from God, (for as to the things which came from God, it was through the Son that they came); and he used the words which I have quoted with reference to the world as framed by God, and not as if all things proceeded from the Father as the Son does. For neither are other things as the Son is, nor is the Word one among those other, for He is Lord and Framer of all; and on this account did the Holy Council declare expressly that He was of the substance of the Father, that we might believe the Word to be other in nature than things which have a beginning, as being alone truly from God; and that no subterfuge should be left open to the impious. This then was the reason why the Council wrote "Of the substance."

28. Again, when the Bishops said that the Word must be described as the True Power and image of the Father as the exact Likeness of the Father in all things, and as unalterable, and as always, and as in Him without division; (for never was the Word not in being, but He was always existing everlastingly with the Father, as the radiance of light), then the party of Eusebius endured it indeed, as not daring to contradict, being put to shame by the arguments which were urged against them; but withal they were caught whispering to each other and winking with their eyes, that "like" and "always," and "the attribute of power," and "in Him," were, as before, common to us and to the Son, and that it was no difficulty to agree to these statements. As to "like," they said

that it is written of us, *Man is the image and glory of God*;[55] "always," that it was written, *For we which live are always*;[56] "In God," *In Him we live and move and have our being*;[57] "unalterable," that it is written, *Nothing shall separate us from the love of Christ*;[58] as to "power," that even the cater-pillar and the locust are called *power* and *great power*,[59] and that it is often said of the people, for instance, *All the power of the Lord came out of the land of Egypt*;[60] and others are heavenly powers, for Scripture says, *The Lord of powers is with us, the God of Jacob is our refuge.*[61] Indeed Asterius, by title the sophist, had said the like in writing, having learned it from them, and before him Arius having learned it also, as has been said. But the Bishops, discerning in this too their simulation, and whereas it is written, *Deceit is in the heart of the impious that imagine evil,*[62] were again compelled on their part to concentrate the sense of the Scriptures, and to re-say and re-write more distinctly still, what they had said before, namely, that the Son is "Consubstantial" with the Father; by way of signifying that the Son is from the

---

[55] 1 Cor 11:7
[56] 2 Cor 4:11
[57] Acts 17:28
[58] Rom 8:35, 38
[59] Joel 2:25
[60] Exod 12:41
[61] Ps 46:7
[62] Prov 12:20

Father, and not merely like, but is the same in likeness, and of showing that the Son's likeness and unalterableness are different from such copy of the same as is ascribed to us, which we acquire from virtuous living and the observance of the commandments.

29. For bodies which are like each other admit of separation and of becoming far off from each other, as are human sons relatively to their parents, (as it is written concerning Adam and Seth who was begotten of him, that he was like him after his own pattern;) but since the generation of the Son from the Father is not according to the nature of men, and He is not only like but also inseparable from the substance of the Father, and He and the Father are One, as He has said Himself, and the Word is ever in the Father and the Father in the Word, as is the radiance relatively to the light, (for this the very term indicates,) therefore the Council, as understanding this, suitably wrote "Consubstantial," that they might both defeat the perverseness of the heretics, and show that the Word was other than created things. For, after thus writing, they at once added, "But they who say that the Son of God is from nothing, or created, or alterable, or a work, or from other substance, these the Holy Catholic Church anathematises." And in saying this, they showed clearly that "Of the substance," and "Consubstantial," do condemn those impious words, "created," and "work," and "brought into being," and "alterable," and "He was not be-

fore His generation." And he who holds these contradicts the Council; but he who does not hold with Arius, must needs hold and enter into the decisions of the Council, suitably regarding them to imply the relation of the radiance to the light, and from thence gaining an image of the sacred truth.

30. Therefore if these men, as their predecessors, make it an excuse that the terms are strange, let them consider the sense in which the Council so wrote, and anathematise what the Council anathematised; and then, if they can, let them find fault with those very terms. For I well know that, if they hold the sense of the Council, they will fully accept the terms in which it is conveyed; whereas if it be the sense which they wish to complain of, all must see that it is idle in them to discuss the wording, when they are but seeking for themselves excuses for a doctrine which is impious.

31. This then was the reason of these words; but if they still complain that such are not scriptural, I observe first, that they have to blame themselves, and no one else in this matter, for it was they who set the example, beginning their war against God with statements not in Scripture; and next, as any one who cares to inquire may easily ascertain, granting that the terms employed by the Council are not absolutely in Scripture, still, as I have said before, they contain the sense of Scripture. Moreover, should they object that to speak of the substance of God is to teach that He is of a

compound nature, (substance implying accidents, and divinity, fatherhood and the like being therefore in the number of certain accidents by which His substance is clad or supplemented,) I reply that the blasphemy, for such it is, is theirs, not ours. For we hold nothing of the kind. This would be to hold that God is material, and that His Son is after all not from His substance, but from a certain attribute or power which is attached to Him. But no; on the contrary, God is transcendently simple, and being such, it follows that in saying "God" and naming "Father," we name nothing besides Him, but we signify His substance or essence Itself. For though to comprehend what the substance of God is be impossible, yet let us only understand of God that He is a Being or Essence, and then, if Scripture indicates Him by means of these names, we too, with the intention of indicating Him and none else, call Him God, and Father, and Lord.

32. When then He says, *I am He that is*, and *I am the Lord God*, or when Scripture says, *God*, we understand nothing else by the words but an intimation of His incomprehensible substance Itself, and that He Is, who is spoken of. Therefore let no one be startled on hearing that the Son of God is from the substance of the Father; rather let him accept the explanation of the Bishops, who in more explicit but equivalent language have for *from God* written "Of the substance." For they considered it the same thing to say that

the Word was *of God* and "of the substance of God," since the word "God," as I have already said, signifies nothing but the substance or essence of *Him who is*. If then the Word is not in such sense from God, as to be Son, genuine and natural, from the Father, but only as creatures are from Him, as being framed, and as *all things are from God*, then neither is He from the substance of the Father, nor again is the Son according to substance Son, but in consequence of virtue, as we who are called sons by grace. But if only He is *from* God, as a genuine Son, as He is, then let the Son, as is reasonable, be called from the substance of God. And the illustration of Light and its Radiance bears the same way. For the sacred writers have not said that the Word was related to God as fire kindled from the heat of the sun, which after a while goes out, for this is an external work and a creature of its author, but they all preach of Him as Radiance, thereby to signify His being from the Divine substance, proper and indivisible, and to express His oneness with the Father. This also will secure His true unalterableness and immutability; for how can these be His, unless He be proper Offspring of the Father's substance? For this too must be taken to confirm His identity with His own Father. And so again, if He be the Word, the Wisdom, the Father's Image, as well as Radiance, on these accounts He plainly must be consubstantial. For unless it be proved that He is not an offspring from God, but an instrument different both in nature and in substance, surely the Council was happy in its wording as well as orthodox in its sense.

33. By this Offspring the Father made all things, and by Him, who is His radiance, diffusing His universal Providence, He exercises His love to men; not as if Light were a simple property lodged in the Son (as perhaps they will say) and only acted through Him, for it is Itself one with the Father, no channel foreign in substance to the Light and to its Fountain, no mere creation; no, this is the belief of Caiaphas and Samosatene, but the Light which is from the Father He possesses in fulness, and of Him others receive according to the measure of each, no intermediate existing between the Father and Him by whom all things have been brought into being. And in Him is the Father revealed and known, and with Him frames the world, and does all things, and is partaken by all things, for all things partake of the Son, as partaking of the Holy Ghost. And these prerogatives of the Son show beyond cavil that He is no creature, but a proper offspring from the Father, as radiance is from light.

Chapter Six

AUTHORITIES IN SUPPORT
OF THE COUNCIL

Theognostus; Dionysius of Alexandria;
Dionysius of Rome; Origen.

34. This then is the intention with which the Fathers who met together at Nicæa made use of these terms; and next, having shown this, I will recur to what I said when I began. I said that at the Council, Eusebius, after objecting to the definition passed by the Fathers assembled, acknowledged that it expressed the Church's faith, as it had come down to us by tradition. I then went on to say that certainly what those who went before us had delivered to us was the true doctrine, and of final authority, and to be followed. However, I thought it best, instead of simply appealing to the voice of Antiquity or of the agreement of Bishops, to explain and defend once more the phrases in which the Council had thought right to convey the Christian Truth. This I have

now done; but I will not bring my letter to an end without giving these heretical teachers specimens of the language of writers of an earlier date, which are in accordance with that to which the Arians take exception.

35. Know then first, O Arians, foes of Christ, that Theognostus, a learned man, did not decline the phrase "Of the substance," for in the second book of his Hypotyposes, he writes thus of the Son:—

Testimony of Theognostus

"The substance of the Son is not any addition from without, brought into the Divine Nature by a fresh creation, but It sprang from the Father's substance, as the radiance of light, as the vapour of water; for neither the radiance, nor the vapour, is the water itself or the sun itself, nor is it alien, but is an effluence of the Father's substance, which, however, suffers no partition. For as the sun remains the same, and is not impaired by the rays poured forth by it, so neither does the Father's substance suffer change, though it has the Son as an Image of Itself."

Theognostus then, after first investigating in the way of an exercise, proceeds to lay down his own sentiments in the foregoing words.

36. Next Dionysius, who was Bishop of Alexandria, upon his writing against Sabellius, and expounding at large the Saviour's economy according to the flesh, and thence

proving against the Sabellians that not the Father but His Word was made flesh, as John has said, was suspected of saying that the Son was a creature and brought into being, and not consubstantial with the Father; on this he writes to his namesake Dionysius, Bishop of Rome, to explain that this was a slander upon him. And he assured him that he had not called the Son a creature, but on the contrary, that he did confess Him to be nothing else than consubstantial. And his words run thus:—

Testimony of Dionysius of Alexandria

"And I have written in another letter a refutation of the false charge they bring against me, that I deny that Christ was consubstantial with God. For though I say that I have not found this term anywhere in Holy Scripture, yet my remarks which follow, and which they have not quoted, are not inconsistent with that belief. For I instanced a human production as being evidently homogeneous, and I observed that undeniably parents differed from their children only in not being simply the same, otherwise there could be neither parents nor children. And my letter, as I said before, owing to present circumstances I am unable to produce; or I would have sent you the very words I used, or rather a copy of the whole, which, if I have an opportunity, I will do still. But my memory is clear that I adduced various parallels of things kindred with each other; for instance, that a plant, grown from seed or from root, was other than that from which it sprang, yet was altogether one in nature with it: and that a stream flowing from a fountain, gained a new name, for that neither the fountain was called stream, nor the stream fountain, and both existed, and the stream was the water from the fountain."

37. And that the Word of God is not a work or creature, but an Offspring proper to the Father's substance and indivisible from it, as the great Council wrote, here you may see in the words of Dionysius, Bishop of Rome, who, while writing against the Sabellians, thus inveighs against those who dared to use their language:—

Testimony of Dionysius of Rome

"Next, I have reason to mention those who separate and tear into portions and destroy that most sacred doctrine of the Church of God, the Divine Monarchy, resolving it into certain three powers and divided subsistences and godheads three. I am told that some of your catechists and teachers of the Divine Word take the lead in this tenet, being in diametrical opposition, so to speak, to Sabellius's opinions; for he blasphemously says that the Son is the Father and the Father the Son, but they in some sort preach three Gods, as dividing the Holy Monad into three subsistences foreign to each other and utterly separate. For it must needs be that with the God of the Universe the Divine Word is united, and the Holy Ghost must repose and habitate in God; thus, in One as in a summit, I mean the God of the Universe, the Omnipotent God, the Divine Triad must of necessity be gathered up and brought together. For it is the doctrine of the presumptuous Marcion, to sever and divide the Divine Monarchy into three origins,—a devil's teaching, not that of Christ's true disciples and lovers of the Saviour's lessons. For these know well that a Triad is preached by divine Scripture, but that neither Old Testament nor New preaches three Gods.

"Equally must we censure those who hold the Son to be a work, and consider that the Lord has come into being, as one of things which really came to be; whereas the divine oracles witness to a generation suitable to Him and becoming, but not to any fashioning or making. A blasphemy then is it, not ordinary, but even the highest, to say that the Lord is in any sort a handiwork. For if He became Son, once He was not; but He was always, if (that is) He be in the Father, as He says Himself, and if the Christ be Word and Wisdom and Power (which, as ye know, divine Scripture says,) and these attributes be powers of God. If then the Son came into being, once these attributes were not; consequently there was a season when God was without them; which is most extravagant. And why treat more on these points to you, men full of the Spirit, and well aware of the extravagances which come into view from saying that the Son is a work?

"Not attending, as I consider, to these, the originators of this opinion have entirely missed the truth, in understanding, contrary to the sense of divine and prophetic Scripture in the passage, the words, *The Lord hath created Me a beginning of His ways unto His works.*[63] For *He created*, as ye know, has various senses; and in this place it must be taken to mean, 'He set Me over the works made by him,' that is, the works 'made by the Son Himself.' And *He created* here must not be taken for *made*, for creating differs from making; *Is not He Thy Father that hath bought thee? hath He not made thee and created thee?*[64] says Moses in his great Song in Deuteronomy. And one may say to them, is He a work, O reckless men, who is *the First-born of every creature, who is born from the womb before the morning star,*[65] who said, as Wisdom, *Before all the hills He begets Me?*[66] And in many passages of the divine oracles is the Son said to have been generated, but not to have come into being, passages which manifestly convict of misconception those men who presume to call His divine and ineffable generation a making.

"Neither then may we divide into three Godheads the wonderful and divine Monad; nor disparage with the name

---

[63] Prov 28:22

[64] Deut 32:6

[65] Col 1:15

[66] Prov 8:25

of 'creature' the dignity and exceeding majesty of the Lord; but we must believe in God the Father Almighty, and in Christ Jesus His Son, and in the Holy Ghost, and hold that to the God of the universe the Word is united. For *I*, says He, *and the Father are One*; and *I in the Father and the Father in Me.*[67] For thus both the Divine Triad, and the holy preaching of the Monarchy will be secured."

38. And concerning the everlasting co-existence of the Word with the Father, and that He is not of another substance or subsistence, but proper to the Father's, as the Bishops in the Council said, hear again from the labour-loving Origen also. For what he has written as if inquiring and exercising himself, that let no one take as expressive of his own sentiments, but of parties who are disputing in the course of investigation; but what he definitely pronounces, that is the sentiment of the labour-loving man. After his disputations then against the heretics, straightway he introduces his personal belief, thus:—

Testimony of Origen

"If there be an Image of the Invisible God, it is an invisible Image; nay, I will be bold to add, that, as being the Likeness of the Father, never was it not. For when was that God,

---

[67] John 14:10, 11

who, according to John, is called Light, (for *God is Light*,[68]) without the Radiance of His proper glory, that a man should presume to assign the Son's beginning of existence, as if He were not before? But when was not in existence that Image of the Father's Ineffable and Indescribable and Unutterable subsistence, that Impress and Word, who alone knows the Father? for let him understand well who dares to say, 'Once the Son was not,' that he is saying, 'Once Wisdom was not,' and 'the Word was not,' and 'Life was not.'"

And again elsewhere he says:—

Another Testimony

"But it is not without sin or peril if because of out weakness of understanding we deprive God, as far as in us lies, of the Only-begotten Word ever co-existing with Him, being the Wisdom in which He rejoiced; else He must be conceived as not always possessed of blessedness."

39. See, we are proving that this view has been transmitted from father to father; but ye, O modern Jews and disciples of Caiaphas, what fathers can ye assign to your phrases? Not one of the understanding and wise; for all abhor you, save the devil alone; none but he is your father in such an apostasy, who both in the beginning scattered on your minds the seeds of this impiety, and now persuades you

---

[68] 1 John 1:5

to slander the Ecumenical Council, for committing to writing, not your doctrines, but that which *from the beginning those who were eye-witnesses and ministers of the Word have handed down to us.*[69] For the faith which the Council has confessed in writing, that is the faith of the Catholic Church; to vindicate this faith, the blessed Fathers so wrote, and thereby condemned the Arian heresy; and this is a chief reason why these men apply themselves to calumniate the Council. For it is not the terms which distress them, but because those terms proved them to be heretics, and daring beyond their fellows.

---

[69] Luke 1:2

A Defense of the Nicene Definition

Chapter Seven

ON THE ARIAN SYMBOL "INGENERATE"

This term afterwards adopted by them; and why; three senses of it. A fourth sense. Ingenerate denotes God in contrast to His creatures, not to His Son; Father the scriptural title instead; Conclusion.

40. AT NICÆA THEN, many years since, their heretical phrases were exposed and anathematised; this has led to their looking for new arguments, and it has issued in their borrowing from the Greeks a weapon for their need, namely, the term "Ingenerate," that by means of it, they may reckon among the things which were made that Word of God, by whom those very things came into being. However it would seem as if they really did not know what the Greeks meant by the term, for the Greek doctrine concerning it in fact tells pointedly against the use to which they put it. The Greeks, let it be observed, after deriving Mind from Good, and the universal Soul from Mind, have no difficulty in calling all three Ingenerate; Mind and Soul as well as Good,

from which Mind and Soul proceed. If then these men must have recourse to heathen writers, let them be quite sure that the said writers make for them; but well I know, they never would have appealed to the Greeks in defence of their heresy, if they had any sanction of it in Scripture; and, as I on my part, have been stating the reason and the meaning with which the Council, and the Fathers earlier than it, defined and committed to writing "Of the substance" and "Consubstantial" agreeably to what Scripture says, so I think I may fairly call upon these Arians to tell us now, if indeed they can, what has led them to this unscriptural term, "Ingenerate," what is the sense in which they consider it to belong to God, and why not to His Son and Word.

41. In truth, I am told that the term has various senses: philosophers say that it means, first, "what has not yet come, but may come, into being; next, what neither has come into being, nor can come; and thirdly, what exists without any birth or becoming, but is everlasting and indestructible." The first sense is nothing to the purpose, nor is the second; it is the third which they endeavour to make available to their purpose, arguing thus: that to be ingenerate is an attribute of God, that to be ingenerate is to be without birth or becoming, but that a Son is born into being. But who does not comprehend the craft of these foes of God? here is a manifest equivocation. It is possible to be ingenerate, that is from eternity, and yet to have an origin, that is, a Father;

in other words, to have a birth and not a becoming, a derivation and yet not a beginning. Even the Greeks, as I have said, hold an eternal derivation. Our Lord is ingenerate as being eternally one with God, generate as being His Son. He has a birth without a becoming.

42. However, the mania of these men is such that they say that a son is generate, and generate means made, and what is made comes "out of nothing;" and what has an origin "is not before its generation," and what is not eternal "once was not." Next, when detected in their sophisms they begin again, after this fashion, that to be ingenerate is to have no author of being, and an author is a maker, and therefore the Son is made, and is one of the creatures. Unthankful, and in truth deaf to the Scriptures, who do everything, and say everything, not to honour God, but to dishonour the Son, ignorant that he who dishonours the Son, dishonours the Father! If He be viewed as Offspring of the substance of the Father, He is of consequence with Him eternally. For this name of Offspring does not detract from the nature of the Word, nor does Ingenerate imply a contrast with the Son, but with the things which come into being through the Son; and as those who address an architect, and call him framer of house or city, do not under this designation include the son who is begotten from him, but on account of the art and science which he displays in his work, call him artificer, signifying thereby that he is not

such as the things made by him, and while they know the nature of the builder, know also that he whom he begets is in nature other than his works; and in regard to his son call him father, but in regard to his works, creator and maker; in like manner he who says that God is ingenerate, invents a name for Him when compared with his works, signifying, not only that He is not brought into being but that He is maker of things which are so brought; yet is aware withal that the Word is other than the things that are made, and alone is a proper Offspring of the Father, through whom all things came to be and consist.

43. In like manner, when the Prophets spoke of God as All-powerful, they did not so name Him, as if the Word were included in that All; (for they knew that the Son was other than things made, and Sovereign over them Himself, by virtue of His likeness to the Father;) but because, while Sovereign over all things which through the Son He has made, God has given the authority of these things to the Son, and having given it, still is Himself as ever, the Lord of all things through Him. Again, when they called God, Lord of hosts, they said not this as if the Word was included in those hosts, but because, while He is Father of the Son, He is Lord of the hosts or powers which through the Son have come to be. And the Word too, as being in the Father, is Himself Lord of them all, and Sovereign over all; for all things, whatsoever the Father hath, are the Son's. This then

being the force of such titles, in like manner let a man call God ingenerate, if it so please him; not however as if the Word were one of things generate or made, but because, as I said before, God not only is not made, but through His proper Word is He the maker of things which are made. For though the Father be specially called Maker, still the Word is the Father's Image and consubstantial with Him; and being His Image, He must be other than creatures altogether; for of whom He is the Image, to Him doth he belong and is like: so that he who calls the Father ingenerate and almighty, perceives in the Ingenerate and the Almighty, His Word and His Wisdom, which is the Son. But these wondrous men, and prone to impiety, hit upon the term Ingenerate, not as caring for God's honour, but from malevolence towards the Saviour; for if they had regard to His honour and worship, it rather had been right and good to acknowledge and to call Him Father, than to give Him this name; for in calling Him ingenerate, they are, as I said before, calling Him strictly from His relation to things which came into being, and simply as a Maker, that so they may imply even the Word to be a work after their own desire; but he who calls God Father, thereby in Him signifies His Son also, and will not fail to understand that, whereas there is a Son, through this Son all things that came into existence were created.

44. I repeat, it will be much more accurate to denote God from the Son, and to call Him Father, than to name

him and call Him Ingenerate from His works merely; for the latter term refers to the works that have been brought into being at the will of God through the Word, but the name of Father betokens the proper Offspring from his substance. And by how much the Word surpasses things made or generate, by so much and more also doth calling God Father surpass the calling Him Ingenerate; for the latter is unscriptural and suspicious, as it has various senses; but the former is simple and scriptural, and more accurate, and alone implies the Son. And "Ingenerate" is a word of the Greeks who know not the Son: but "Father" has been acknowledged and vouchsafed to us by our Lord; for He, Himself, knowing whose Son He was, said, *I in the Father and the Father in Me*;[70] and, *He that hath seen Me hath seen the Father*;[71] and, *I and the Father are one*;[72] but nowhere is He found to call the Father Ingenerate. Moreover, when He teaches us to pray, He says not, "When ye pray, say, O God Ingenerate," but rather *When ye pray say, Our Father, who art in heaven.*[73]

45. Moreover, it was His Will, that the compendium of our faith should look the same way. For He has bid us be baptised, not into the name of the Ingenerate and gener-

---

[70] John 14:10, 11
[71] John 14:9
[72] John 10:30
[73] Matt 6:9

ate, not into the name of Uncreate and creature, but into the name of Father, Son, and Holy Ghost; for with such an initiation we also are made sons verily, and, while using the name of the Father, we acknowledge from that name, the Word in the Father. But if He wills that we should call His own Father our Father, we must not on that account measure ourselves with the Son according to nature, for it is because of the Son that the Father is so called by us; for since the Word bore our body and in us came to be, therefore, by reason of the Word in us, is God called our Father. For the Spirit of the Word in us, addresses through us His own Father as ours, which is the Apostle's meaning when he says, *God hath sent forth the Spirit of His Son into your hearts, crying, Abba, Father.*[74]

46. So much on the term "Ingenerate," which admits indeed of a pious use, but, in the hands of Christ's foes, has but covered them with shame, as did their words and deeds at the beginning. How the Council, then assembled at Nicæa, met them, with what prudence and with what fidelity to Holy Scripture and the Fathers, I have related and explained to the best of my powers; but I cannot hope that those restless spirits will give up their opposition now any more than then. They will doubtless run about in search of other pretences, and of others again after those. When, in

---

[74] Gal 4:6

the Prophet's words, will *the Ethiopian change his skin or the leopard his spots?*[75] Thou, however, Beloved, on receiving this, read it by thyself; and, if thou approvest of it, read it also to the brethren, who are with thee, that they too, on hearing it, may respond to the Council's zeal for the truth and for doctrinal exactness, and may reprobate the heresy and the controversial devices of the Arian faction; because to God, even the Father, is due the glory, honour, and worship, with His co-unoriginate Son and Word, together with the All-holy and life-giving Spirit, now and unto endless ages of ages. Amen.

---

[75] Jer 13:23

LETTER OF EUSEBIUS OF CAESAREA
TO THE PEOPLE OF HIS DIOCESE

47. WHAT WAS TRANSACTED concerning the Faith of the Church at the Great Council assembled at Nicæa, you have probably learned, Beloved, from other quarters, rumour being wont to precede the accurate account of what is doing. But lest in such reports the circumstances of the case should have been misrepresented to you, we have thought it necessary to transmit to you, first, the formula of faith presented by ourselves, and then, the second, which the Fathers put forth with some additions to our words. Our own formula then, which was read in the presence of our most pious Emperor, and declared to be good and unexceptionable, ran thus:—

48. "As we have received from the Bishops who preceded us, and in our first catechisings, and when we received Holy Baptism, and as we have learned from the divine Scriptures, and as we believed and taught when in the order of presby-

ters, and in the Episcopate itself, so believing also at the time present, we report to you our faith, and it is this:—

Creed of Eusebius

"We believe in One God, the Father Almighty, the Maker of all things visible and invisible.

"And in one Lord Jesus Christ, the Word of God, God from God, Light from Light, Life from Life, Son Only-begotten, first-born of every creature, before all the ages begotten from the Father, through whom also all things were made; who for our salvation was made flesh, and lived among men, and suffered and rose again the third day, and ascended to the Father, and will come again in glory to judge quick and dead.

"And we believe also in one Holy Ghost; believing each of These to be and to exist, the Father truly Father, and the Son truly Son, and the Holy Ghost truly Holy Ghost; as also our Lord, sending forth His disciples for the preaching, said, *Go, teach all the nations, baptising them in the Name of the Father, and of the Son, and of the Holy Ghost.*[76] Concerning whom we confidently affirm that so we hold and so we think, and so we have held aforetime, and that we maintain this faith unto the death, anathematising every godless heresy. That this we have ever thought from our heart and soul, from the time

---

[76] Matt 28:19

we recollect ourselves, and now think and say in truth, before God Almighty and our Lord Jesus Christ do we bear witness, being able by proofs to show and to convince you that also in times past such was our belief and such our preaching."

49. On this faith being publicly put forth by us, no room for contradiction appeared to any one; but our most pious Emperor himself before any one else, testified that it comprised most orthodox statements. He confessed moreover, that such were his own sentiments, and he exhorted all present to agree to it, and to subscribe its articles and to assent to the same, with the insertion of the single word, "Consubstantial," which moreover he interpreted as not in the sense of the affections of bodies, nor as if the Son subsisted from the Father in the way of division or any severance; for that the immaterial, and intellectual, and incorporeal Nature could not be the subject of any corporeal affection, but that it became us to conceive of such things in a divine and ineffable manner. And such were the theological remarks of our most wise and most religious Emperor; on which the Bishops, with a view to the addition of Consubstantial, drew up the following formula:—

Nicene Creed

"We believe in One God, the Father Almighty, Maker of all things visible and invisible:—

"And in One Lord Jesus Christ, the Son of God, begotten of the Father, Only-begotten, that is, from the Substance of the Father; God from God, Light from Light, Very God from Very God, begotten not made, consubstantial with the Father, by whom all things were made, both things in heaven and things in earth; who for us men and for our salvation came down and was made flesh, was made man, suffered, and rose again the third day, ascended into heaven, and cometh to judge quick and dead.

"And in the Holy Ghost.

"But those who say, 'Once He was not,' and 'Before His generation He was not,' and 'He came into being from nothing,' or those who pretend that the Son of God is 'Of other subsistence or substance,' or 'created,' or 'alterable,' or 'mutable,' the Catholic Church anathematises."

50. On their dictating this formula, we did not let it pass without inquiry in what sense they introduced "Of the substance of the Father," and "consubstantial with the Father." Accordingly questions and explanations took place, and the meaning of the words underwent the scrutiny of reason. And they professed, that the phrase "Of the substance" was indicative of the Son's being indeed from the Father, yet without being as if a part of Him. And with this understanding we thought good to assent to the sense of such religious doctrine, teaching, as it did, that the Son was from the Father, not however a part of His substance. On this account we assented to this sense ourselves, without

declining even the term "Consubstantial," peace being the object which we set before us, and maintenance of the orthodox view.

51. In the same way we also admitted "Begotten, not made;" since the Council alleged that "made" was an appellative common to the other creatures which came to be through the Son, to whom the Son had no likeness. Therefore, it was said, He was not a work resembling the things which through Him came to be, but was of a substance which is above the level of any work, and which the Divine oracles teach to have been generated from the Father, the mode of generation being inscrutable and incomprehensible to every created nature.

52. And so too on examination there are grounds for saying, that the Son is "consubstantial" with the Father; not in the way of bodies, nor like mortal beings, for He is not consubstantial by division of substance, or by severance, no nor by any affection, or changing, or alteration of the Father's substance and attributes (since from all such the ingenerate nature of the Father is alien), but because "consubstantial with the Father" suggests that the Son of God bears no resemblance to the creatures which have been made, but that He is in every way after the pattern of His Father alone who begat Him, and that He is not of any other subsistence and substance, but from the Father. To which term also, thus interpreted, it appeared well to assent; since we were aware

that even among the ancients, some learned and illustrious bishops and writers have used the term "consubstantial" in their theological teaching concerning the Father and Son.

53. So much then be said concerning the Faith which has been published; to which all of us assented, not without inquiry, but according to the specified senses, mentioned in the presence of the most religious Emperor himself, and justified by the forementioned considerations. And as to the anathematism published by the Fathers at the end of the Faith, it did not trouble us, because it forbade to use words not in Scripture, from which almost all the confusion and disorder of the Church has come. Since then no divinely inspired Scripture has used the phrases, "Out of nothing," and "Once He was not," and the rest which follow, there appeared no ground for using or teaching them; to which also we assented as a good decision, since it had not been our custom hitherto to use these terms.

54. Moreover to anathematise "Before his generation He was not," did not seem preposterous, in that it is confessed by all, that the Son of God was before the generation according to the flesh. Nay, our most religious Emperor did at the time prove in a speech, that even according to His divine generation which is before all ages, He was in being, since even before He was generated in act, He was in virtue with the Father ingenerately, the Father being always Father, as King always, and Saviour always, being all things

in virtue, and having all things in the same respects and in the same way.

55. This we have been forced to transmit to you, Beloved, as making clear to you the deliberateness of our inquiry and assent, and how reasonably we resisted even to the last minute as long as we were offended at statements which differed from our own, but received without contention what no longer troubled us, as soon as, on a candid examination of the sense of the words, they appeared to us to coincide with what we ourselves had professed in the Faith which we had already published.

A Defense of the Nicene Definition

Printed in Great Britain
by Amazon